# Meet the Quokkas!

By Caryn Jenner

**Senior Editor** Carrie Love
**Project Editor** Kritika Gupta
**Art Editors** Mohd Zishan, Polly Appleton
**Jacket Co-ordinator** Issy Walsh
**Jacket Designer** Dheeraj Arora
**DTP Designers** Dheeraj Singh, Nand Kishore Acharya
**Project Picture Researcher** Sakshi Saluja
**Producer, pre-production** Tony Phipps
**Senior producer** Ena Matagic
**Managing Editors** Penny Smith, Monica Saigal
**Deputy Managing Art Editor** Ivy Sengupta
**Managing Art Editor** Mabel Chan
**Delhi Team Head** Malavika Talukder
**Publishing Manager** Francesca Young
**Creative Director** Helen Senior
**Publishing Director** Sarah Larter

**Reading Consultant** Jacqueline Harris
**Subject Consultant** Kim Bryan

First published in Great Britain in 2020 by
Dorling Kindersley Limited
80 Strand, London, WC2R 0RL

A CIP catalogue record for this book is available from the British Library.
ISBN: 978-0-2414-1388-3
Printed and bound in China

The publisher would like to thank the following for their kind permission to reproduce their photographs:
(Key: a-above; b-below/bottom; c-centre; f-far; l-left; r-right; t-top)

**1 Dreamstime.com:** Kitchner Bain. **3 Dreamstime.com:** Ashley Whitworth (br). **4–5 Getty Images:** Sarah Lewis / Moment RF. **6–7 Dreamstime.com:** Adwo. **8 Dreamstime.com:** Alfotokunst (br); Oliver Neumann (c). **9 Getty Images:** Posnov. **10 Dreamstime.com:** Johnny Lye. **11 Alamy Stock Photo:** Avalon / Photoshot License (b). **12 iStockphoto.com:** J_Knaupe (b). **14 Dreamstime.com:** Lizgiv (bl); Wiritjiribin (br). **15 iStockphoto.com:** JohnCarnemolla. **16 Dreamstime.com:** Andrey Moisseyev. **17 Alamy Stock Photo:** Gekko Studios. **18–19 Alamy Stock Photo:** mauritius images GmbH. **20 Alamy Stock Photo:** Frans Lanting Studio. **21 Alamy Stock Photo:** Bill Bachman (cla). **Dreamstime.com:** Artistrobd (cr). **SuperStock:** Animals Animals (clb). **23 Alamy Stock Photo:** Avico Ltd. **24 SuperStock:** Kevin Schafer / Minden Pictures (t). **25 naturepl.com:** Kevin Schafer. **26–27 Alamy Stock Photo:** Avalon / Photoshot License. **28 Alamy Stock Photo:** Kitch Bain (b). **29 Dreamstime.com:** Peter Galleghan (t). **30 Dreamstime.com:** Ozflash (b). **31 naturepl.com:** Kevin Schafer. **32–33 Alamy Stock Photo:** Avalon / Photoshot License. **34 Alamy Stock Photo:** Avalon / Photoshot License (b). **35 Getty Images:** John Crux Photography. **36–37 Alamy Stock Photo:** Angus McComiskey. **38 Dreamstime.com:** Barbro Rutgersson. **39 iStockphoto.com:** Totajla (b). **40 Getty Images:** Greg Wood / AFP (b). **41 Getty Images:** Schafer & Hill. **42 Dreamstime.com:** Tmyra (clb). **43 Dreamstime.com:** Adam9277 (cl); David Steele (tr, br).

**Endpapers:** Front: **Alamy Stock Photo:** Avalon / Photoshot License. Back: **Alamy Stock Photo:** Avalon / Photoshot License.

**Cover images:** Front: **Dreamstime.com:** Oliver Neumann c; Back: **Dreamstime.com:** Lizgiv cla.

All other images © Dorling Kindersley
For further information see: www.dkimages.com

A WORLD OF IDEAS:
**SEE ALL THERE IS TO KNOW**

**www.dk.com**

# Contents

# Chapter 1
# Meet the quokkas

Look at these animals. Do you see the smiles on their furry faces?

These animals are quokkas [KWOK-ahs]. A quokka looks like it is smiling because its mouth turns up at the ends. That's why quokkas are called the happiest animals in the world.

Quokkas are mammals that live in Australia.

A quokka is about the size of a house cat. It has a chubby body with thick, brown fur. Its tail is thin, like a rat's tail.

A quokka has big back paws and small front paws. Watch out! It also has sharp claws.

Quokkas can weigh up to 4.2 kg (9 lbs).

A quokka's face looks friendly. Its ears are round like a teddy bear's ears. It has dark eyes and a big, black nose. Plus there's the happy quokka smile!

Quokkas spend most of their time in shrubs and undergrowth.

A joey stays in its mother's pouch for up to six and a half months.

A female quokka has a
special pouch on her tummy.
This is where she keeps her baby.
A baby quokka is called a joey.
See the little joey peeking out
of its pouch? Peepo!

Quokkas usually have one baby at a time,
but sometimes they have twins.

# Where do quokkas live?

Quokkas live in Australia. Most quokkas now live on Rottnest Island off the coast of Australia. There aren't many quokkas left on the mainland.

Rottnest Island is home to about 10,000 quokkas.

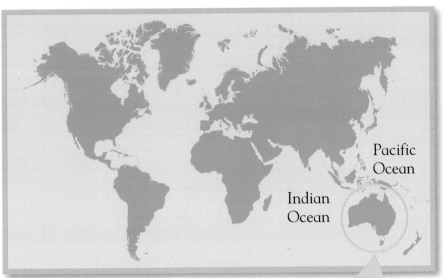

Pacific
Ocean

Indian
Ocean

Australia lies between the
Indian and Pacific Oceans.

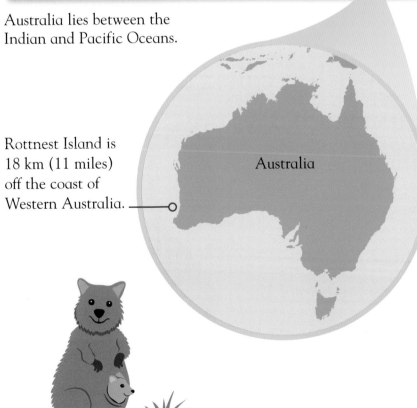

Rottnest Island is
18 km (11 miles)
off the coast of
Western Australia.

Australia

# Chapter 2
# Pals with pouches

An animal that keeps its baby
in a pouch is called a marsupial.
Marsupial babies are
called joeys.

Quokka

Red-necked
wallaby

What other animals keep their joeys in a pouch? Wallabies and kangaroos do. A quokka is a kind of wallaby. Kangaroos and wallabies live in Australia.

Red kangaroo

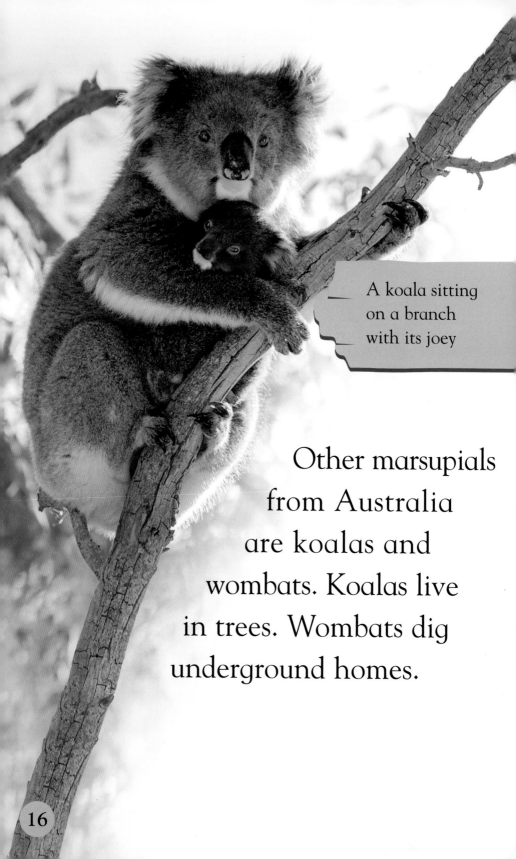

A koala sitting on a branch with its joey

Other marsupials from Australia are koalas and wombats. Koalas live in trees. Wombats dig underground homes.

A mother wombat keeps her joey in a pouch near her tail. The pouch faces backwards. That way it doesn't fill with dirt when the mother is digging.

A Common wombat mother curls up with her joey

Another kind of marsupial is the opossum. Opossums live in North and South America. A mother opossum looks after lots of joeys in her pouch.

When the joeys grow too big
for the pouch, they hold onto
their mother's fur.

A Virginia opossum
carrying babies on
her back

19

# Mad about marsupials

There are more than 330 different kinds of marsupials. Here are some of them.

**Red kangaroo**
A red kangaroo is the largest marsupial.

### Numbat
A numbat catches insects with its long, sticky tongue.

### Tasmanian devil
A Tasmanian devil makes an awful smell when it's stressed.

### Water opossum
A water opossum is the only marsupial that can swim.

# Chapter 3
# Growing up

A newborn quokka joey is only about the size of a raisin. The tiny joey stays safe and warm in its mother's pouch. It feeds on its mother's milk. It doesn't look like a quokka until it gets older.

A young joey inside
its mother's pouch

Joey peeping out of its mother's pouch

Soon the quokka joey grows fur.
It pokes its head out of its mother's
pouch and looks around.

After about six months, the joey climbs out of the pouch for the first time. It's ready to explore!

After about eight months, the quokka joey grows too big for its mother's pouch. It can find its own food.

A quokka mother and baby on Rottnest Island, Australia

Soon it will be all grown up. It may stay with its mother until it is about 20 months old.

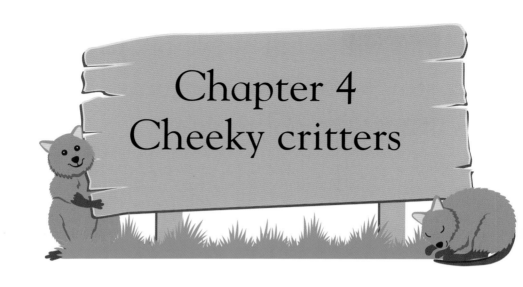

# Chapter 4
# Cheeky critters

Hop, hop, hop! Quokkas hop about on their big back paws. Sometimes, they move around on all four paws.

A quokka sleeping with its head between its legs

Quokkas are usually active at night. During the day, they find shelter from the hot sun. They fall asleep in the shade.

Quokkas eat grass and leaves, and stems of shrubs and bushes. They climb up small bushes and trees. They pull down the branches with their sharp claws and eat the leaves.

Sometimes, there is no food. Then the quokka gets energy from fat stored in its tail.

Quokka eating a leaf

Quokkas live near streams and swamps. They drink the water. They also take water from the plants they eat.

A quokka jumps across a stream

Sometimes, quokkas make trails to help them to get from place to place.

The quokkas on Rottnest Island live near people. Visitors come to the island especially to see the quokkas. They take lots of photos. Quokkas are not afraid of people. They are friendly creatures, but they are still wild animals. They might bite!

Quokkas being photographed by a visitor

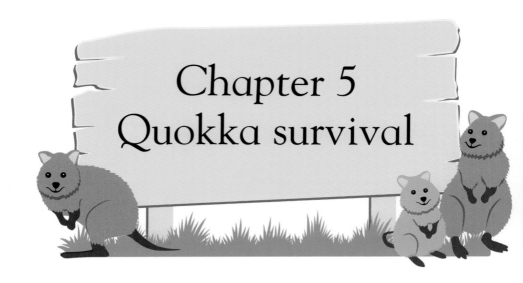

# Chapter 5
# Quokka survival

About 10,000 quokkas live on the small island of Rottnest. These lucky quokkas don't have to worry about other animals hunting them. That is one reason there are so many.

Quokkas are very popular on Rottnest Island. As quokkas are wild, people are not allowed to touch them or feed them.

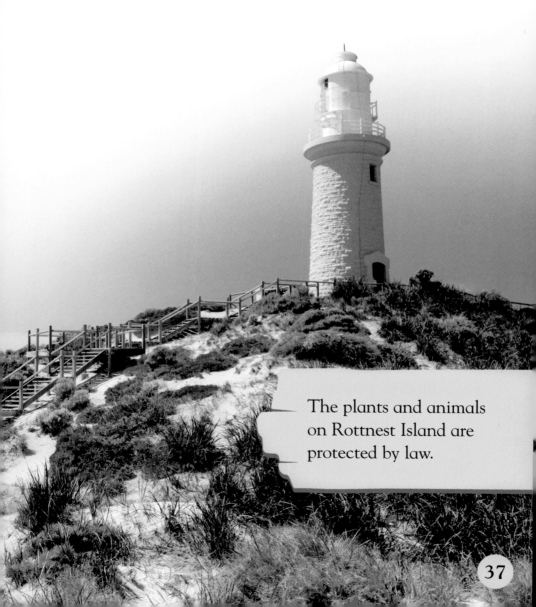

The plants and animals on Rottnest Island are protected by law.

Foxes are not native to Australia. They were taken to the country in the mid-1800s to be hunted.

There used to be lots of quokkas on mainland Australia, too. Sadly, there aren't many left there now. Animals such as foxes and cats hunt them. People build roads and buildings on the quokkas' habitat and destroy it. Large bush fires also destroy the quokkas' habitat.

Quokkas have lost much of their habitat on mainland Australia due to bush fires and deforestation.

Quokkas are in danger of dying out on mainland Australia. People there are trying to help the quokkas. They are protecting the quokkas' habitat so it doesn't disappear completely. Hopefully, the quokkas will keep smiling for a long time to come.

An orphaned quokka joey in Australia

# Quick quokka facts

Quokkas belong to the "macropod" animal family. Macropod means "big foot". Kangaroos are also macropods. Here are more quick quokka facts.

Quokkas live to be about ten years old in the wild.

Human food can make quokkas sick.

The name "quokka" is an Aboriginal word.

An explorer to Rottnest Island thought the quokkas were giant rats! He named the island Rottnest, meaning "rat's nest".

# Quiz

**(1)** Why does a quokka look like it's smiling?

**(2)** How much does a quokka weigh?

**(3)** What is a joey?

**(4)** Where does a female quokka keep her baby?

**(5)** Where do quokkas live?

**(6)** Quokkas and koalas are marsupials. Can you name two other marsupials in this book?

**7** When does a joey get too big to fit in its mother's pouch?

**8** When are quokkas usually active?

**9** Where does a quokka get energy from when it can't find food?

**10** How many quokkas live on Rottnest Island?

45

# Glossary

**Aboriginal**
Relating to the first people who lived in Australia.

**deforestation**
Cutting down trees over a large area by humans.

**habitat**
Where an animal or plant lives.

**macropod**
The family of animals that includes quokkas, wallabies and kangaroos.

**mammal**
A warm-blooded animal that produces milk to feed its young.

**marsupial**
A type of mammal. Most females have a pouch in which their young live.

**native**
Relating to an animal or plant that occurs naturally in a place.

**swamp**
Low-lying wet ground also known as a bog.

# Index

# A LEVEL FOR EVERY READER

This book is a part of an exciting four-level reading series to support children in developing the habit of reading widely for both pleasure and information. Each book is designed to develop a child's reading skills, fluency, grammar awareness and comprehension in order to build confidence and enjoyment when reading.

> ### Ready for a Level 2 (Beginning to Read) book
> A child should:
> - be able to recognize a bank of common words quickly and be able to blend sounds together to make some words.
> - be familiar with using beginner letter sounds and context clues to figure out unfamiliar words.
> - sometimes correct his/her reading if it doesn't look right or make sense.
> - be aware of the need for a slight pause at commas and a longer one at full stops.

### A valuable and shared reading experience

For many children, reading requires much effort, but adult participation can make reading both fun and easier. Here are a few tips on how to use this book with a young reader:

*Check out the contents together:*
- read about the book on the back cover and talk about the contents page to help heighten interest and expectation.
- discuss new or difficult words.
- chat about labels, annotations and pictures.

*Support the reader:*
- tell the child the title and help them predict what the book will be about.
- give the book to the young reader to turn the pages.
- where necessary, encourage longer words to be broken into syllables, sound out each one and then flow the syllables together; ask him/her to reread the sentence to check the meaning.
- encourage the reader to vary his/her voice as he/she reads; demonstrate how to do this if helpful.

*Talk at the end of each page:*
- ask questions about the text and the meaning of some of the words used – this helps develop comprehension skills.
- read the quiz at the end of the book and encourage the reader to answer the questions, if necessary, by turning back to the relevant pages to find the answers.